The Blooming Petals

A collection of petals that unfolded through storms, darkness, and unfavorable weather- each one carrying a story of how I bloomed when life tried to break me.

Jayasree Itty

/ BookLeaf
Publishing

India | USA | UK

Made with ❤ on the BookLeaf Publishing Platform
www.bookleafpub.in
www.bookleafpub.com

Dedication

To every soul who has walked through the storm
and still chosen to bloom—
to those who carried unseen battles,
yet held on to love like a fragile light.

To the women who were told to stay quiet,
but found poetry in their pain;
to the mothers who forgot themselves
while nurturing the world;
to the dreamers who fell,
but rose again with trembling hands.

And to the petals of my own life —
each scar, each tear, each prayer —
for teaching me that even the most fragile bloom
can rise from the thorns and still smell of hope.

Preface

The Blooming Petals is a collection born from moments of silence, pain, and quiet resilience. Each poem is a reflection of my inner journey — from the wounds that once bled unseen to the strength that slowly blossomed through faith, love, and self-discovery.

These poems are not just words; they are pieces of my soul gathered from nights of reflection, prayers whispered in solitude, and the unspoken emotions of a woman who learned to rise after every fall.

Through The Blooming Petals, I wish to remind every heart that healing is not a destination but a process — a gentle unfolding, like petals opening after a long storm. Each verse carries the fragrance of hope, the warmth of endurance, and the light of becoming.

If my words can touch even one soul, ease one heart, or help someone find beauty in their own brokenness, this book has fulfilled its purpose.

Acknowledgements

My heartfelt gratitude to the **Divine Presence** that guided me through every silence and storm, teaching me that healing begins with faith.

To my husband, **Vinuvettan**, thank you for your patience, love, and quiet strength — your support gave me the courage to keep believing in myself.

To my son, **Devarsh**, you are the light that made me rediscover hope and purpose. Every word I write carries your reflection — gentle, pure, and full of life.

To my **Mother**, whose prayers became my protection, and to my siblings and loved ones, thank you for your constant encouragement.

Finally, my gratitude to **BookLeafPublishing** for giving The Blooming Petals a home in the world.

This book is for every soul who has walked through pain and still chose to bloom.

1. The Unhealed Wounds

Every time I bleed when I hear your name,
the scar still whispers — a scratch that never healed.

"You should forget, you should move on,"
they say, as if time can wash away a soul.

Yes, memories may fade like mist,
yet this bleeding scar stays — eternal, unseen.

Am I bleeding upon rejection?
No —
I'm bleeding upon the unseen worth of myself.
The wound still burns,
but from its fire I rise —
not healed,
but whole enough to shine.

2. I was Here All Along

I have waited for your voice
while I was steeping into the silence.

I have waited for your touch
while I collapsed beneath the struggles.

I have waited for your light
amidst the moments of chaos.

And when the silence deepened,
I felt you in my breath —
not as thunder or miracle,
but as calm within the storm,
a whisper saying,
"I was here all along."

3. The Woman

You are the iron, forged through the fire of struggles.

You are the strength, revealed through striking storms.

You are the root that holds your family through the darkness.

You are the fire that burns yourself to become the light.
And when the world looks for miracles,

they find you —
the woman who became.

4. Until He comes

You were the most trusted soul —
and you shattered that trust.
She believed you would guard her dreams,
but you turned them into dust.

You crushed a blooming flower,
her still-unfolding petals
beneath the weight of your desire.
You laughed —
and her voice faded into silence.

Since then, she hides
within the quiet folds of her trauma,
where nights whisper
what her lips no longer tell.

Until he comes —
the one who sees her beyond the scars,
who loves her for the woman she is,
who beholds the light she forgot she owned —
and in his gaze,
she meets the reflection
of her own rebirth.

5. The Ray of Hope

You were there till I found you—
while I was grieving,
buried beneath the dust of my past.
You waited, unseen and unacknowledged,
a quiet flame beneath the ashes.

And one day,
when the dust of worries was finally swept away,
I saw you through a new window—
the life I once believed was lost.
You were there all along,
till I found you
my love.

6. Petrichor

The earthy smell took me back to my younger self.
She stood there, hands unfolded, waiting to catch the
rain.

The gentle breeze brushed through her hair,
and the dripping rhythm of raindrops
soothed her curious ears.

The soft touch of running water
tickled her bare feet,
as puddles mirrored her laughter.
Somewhere between those drops and giggles,
I found the part of me I thought I'd lost —
the girl who believed the sky spoke to her
through rain.

7. Homesick Mornings

She looked through the window —
the buildings stood tall,
pointing toward the horizon.
Vehicles moved like ants,
each rushing for life.
No one paused to look at another.

It has been the same for years —
the same busy morning,
the same horns,
the same bleating of engines.
And yet, somewhere deep within,
she longed for the mornings of her village —
the sound of temple bells,
the scent of wet soil after rain,
the echo of rooster calls from far-off fields.

Now, the window holds nothing but dust —like her heart,
covered with dusted ambitions,
longing for a breeze that smells of home.

8. Amma

One who taught us resilience
and how to be strong in the midst of heaviness.

One who taught us the power of prayer and how to find
peace within the storm.

One who taught us how to be happy
and how to smile through the rain of sadness.

One who taught us unconditional love
and how to give without measure.

One who taught us unwavering faith
and how to live with love and grace.

Amma,
you have always been a woman
who discovered strength through struggles,
and turned every wound
into a blossom of courage.

9. Returning to My Roots

I thought I had lost my strength,
but the earth that raised me
had been keeping it safe all along.

Here, the rain smells like memory,
the winds whisper my name softly,
and every corner carries
a fragment of who I used to be.

I came back to heal,
but instead I found power —
the kind that grows quietly,
like roots beneath the soil,
holding me steady
for everything yet to bloom.

10. Whispers of the Night

The night is calm,
and the breeze rushes toward her window —
as if someone longed to talk with her.

She opens the window
to the nature that has always nurtured her.
Beneath the starry sky,
she sees a world wrapped in happiness and peace.

The moon winks at her in awe,
and the stars light up her glow.
She opens her heart once more
to the nature that once healed
the wounds of a little girl.
And through the rustle of leaves
comes a whisper —
"Where have you been, dear?
We missed you..."

She closes her eyes,
feeling the warmth of the wind,
and whispers back,
"I have been here — lost and missed...
and now, found myself."

11. Life-The Relentless Teacher

Life is a relentless teacher,
weaving her lessons through our struggles.
At times, she arrives as a storm,
washing away all that must be gone.

At times, she burns like fire,
forging us until we gleam — radiant and raw.
Then she becomes the water,
smoothing our edges
until we are gentle enough to hold love again.

Her lessons never end.
Yet, with time, the soul learns
to cradle each lesson as it was meant to be.
And when we turn back,
we see — her touch was never to crush,
but to chisel the soul
for the path it was born to walk

12. Rainy Night

It's a rainy night —
the dripping sound of rain soothes my ears.
The windowpanes are cracking,
frogs are crying,
and crickets are creaking.

I always wish you were here beside me —
to listen to the music of the rain,
to feel the damp breeze on our faces,
to breathe in the scent of the wet earth we both adore.

A cool calm spreads through my heart,
and I know you would have smiled too —
for nights like this are meant
for two hearts that find peace in nature's song.

13. My Little Miracle

I was dizzy and worn,
yet I managed — just to see you.
I was afraid and tense,
yet I managed — just to kiss you.
Through sleepless nights and aching bones,
I managed — just to feel you.
In the haze of confusion and panic,
I managed — just to hold you close.

I was all these and more...
yet I managed — only to reach
for your tiny, trembling paws,
my little miracle —
the reason I breathe, the proof
I endured.

14. Tears of Gratitude

I still remember the nights I cried for you —
not out of weakness,
but out of love too deep for words.

I feared the silence,
I feared the unknown,
and yet, through it all,
you taught me the language of patience.

Now I see you —
growing, blooming, finding your light —
and my tears return,
but this time, they are prayers of gratitude.

You have always been my lesson in faith,
my reason to believe
that miracles don't arrive suddenly —
they grow quietly,
just like you.

15. His Sun

The storm rose within me —
a weary tide of love and ache.
My words, sharp for a moment,
fell heavy between us.

He looked up,
eyes wide like dawn after rain,
and asked,
"Amma is sad?"

The world stilled.
How could such a tender voice
untangle every knot inside me?
I gathered my breath,
smiled through the mist,
and said softly,
"No, Amma is happy."

And that was enough —
for my smile became his sun,
my calm, his world.
He needed no perfection,
only to feel that love still lived
beneath the silence after the storm.

16. A Prayer for My Son

I wish you to cherish every moment,
to see wonder in the smallest things —
a fluttering leaf, a morning breeze,
a smile that needs no reason.

I wish you to be protected by the angels,
their wings wrapping you in light
when the world feels too heavy to hold.

I wish you to find happiness —
not in what you own,
but in who you become.

I wish you to be loved by everyone,
and more than that,
to love yourself without doubt.

I wish you to be strong enough
to hold everything that comes your way —
the storms, the silences,
the dreams yet to unfold.

I wish you to be happy —
truly, deeply, endlessly —

for your smile is my sunrise,
and your peace, my prayer.

17. Divine voice

Oh my child,
I know you are suffering through heartbreak —
but why,
when you have me to heal your wound?

You are walking through loneliness —
but why,
when I have never left your side?

You cry through the long nights —
but why,
when my love waits to wipe your tears?

And where are you searching for me?
I am here, within you.

In every breath,
in every heartbeat,
in the quiet between your tears —
I am the love you seek.
Turn to me,
and find yourself again.

18. The Blooming Petals

Why me?
What should I do?
Whispered a thousand times...

A tug of war —
between escape and craving.

And finally,
a voice — clearer, straighter:
"You are abundant enough."

The wings of her life unfold —
and she begins to fly...
Fly above them all.

19. To My tomorrow

I want you to be strong and healthy,
to walk through storms with calm eyes.

I want you to be peaceful and happy,
to smile without reason,
to rest without guilt.

I want you to be the one who evolved —
soft yet unbreakable,
rooted in quiet confidence.

I want you to find meaning
even in the smallest bloom,
and strength in every scar.

I want you to be the one who survived —
not just the battles,
but the loneliness between them.

And when you look back,
may you whisper to your yesterdays,
"Thank you for not giving up."

20. Where My Soul Feels Home

The temple hymns rise with the dawn,
weaving through the trees,
calling something ancient in me awake.

The wind brushes past my face,
like a mother's palm that knows no words,
only warmth.

The cuckoo sings from somewhere unseen,
and I smile —
some songs don't need to be found,
only felt.

And when night falls,
its lullaby folds me into peace —
reminding me that healing
was never in running away,
but in returning
to where
my soul feels home.

21. Healed

She took the pen
trembled, shivered —
an echo whispered,
"You are not genuine,
you are not authentic."

The words kept flowing down,
pulling her back
to the day
when she was young and raw.

There she stood —
a shattered mirror,
irretrievable.

"Did you copy the words?
Aren't you ashamed?"
The questions pierced her
like arrows.
The mentor she trusted to understand
became the voice that broke her.
And the little sheep bled
upon the thorns
of self-worth and embarrassment.

Years passed,
and the girl turned into a woman,
circling through the realities of life.
Then came a call from her soul —
to suffer, to break,
and to heal.
To heal, to write —
and through every word,
to finally forgive
the girl who once trembled.

22. She Rose Softly

Once she stood — a statue of silence,
breathless, still, without life's glow.
Her eyes held oceans of unspoken fear,
her cheeks, as barren as droughted earth.
Her trembling hands carved words
from the ache of her own being.

She was doubtful, lonely,
tired and quietly breaking —
yet beneath that wounded heart,
a spark slept,
like water buried beneath a mountain's weight.

And one day,
that spark rose —
softly, fiercely, endlessly —
turning her stillness into **bloom**.

www.ingramcontent.com/pod-product-compliance
Lightning Source LLC
Chambersburg PA
CBHW051001030426
42339CB00007B/437